Nina Lemon

Losing It

A Play about Coming Together and Falling Apart

With music & additional lyrics by Lisa Von H

Salamander Street

PLAYS

First published in 2020 by Salamander Street Ltd.
(info@salamanderstreet.com)

Losing It © Nina Lemon, 2020

Song lyrics © Lisa Von H, 2020

ISBN: 9781913630560

Printed and bound in Great Britain

10 9 8 7 6 5 4 3 2 1

This play was developed working directly with young people as part of my role as Artistic Director of youth arts charity Peer Productions. I would like to acknowledge the charity's executive and trustee team, particularly Managing Director Ed Simpson, for bringing this work to such a large audience. I am indebted to all the young people who shared their stories with me with such candour. I would also like to thank the original cast Simran Bhandari, Elissa Cooper, Chloe Ching, Jess Hearn, Sophie Maher, Agata Nielsen, Oliver Parsons, Jamie Patterson, Daniel Pirie, Megan Raynor, Luke Rose, Amber Wadey, Jas Woods and Esme Wright for their support and integrity in the development of the play and the many other young casts who have since taken this play out on tour.

This play is designed with flexible casting in mind to suit casts from 12 actors to 24+.

Minimum cast requirements are 12 – 7 female, 4 male and 1 actor to play Ash*

*Ash is assigned female at birth. He realises he is trans when he is a teenager and adopts male pronouns and changes his name from Natasha to Ash. We see the character from age 11 when they are assumed female through to age 18 when they are confident in their gender identity.

Various doubling options are possible. For minimum sized cast the following doubling can work.

POPPY
ROB
MADDIE/POLICE W
MIKE/POLICE M
CHARLOTTE
ASH
SEREN
TIM/POPPY'S DAD
SALLY/TIM'S MUM
MELANIE/CARYL
DAVID/DANNO
LUCY/MAXINE (with quick changes)

The play was designed to be performed as one act with a running time of 85 mins.
If an interval is required, it could be placed between scenes 14 and 15.

To listen to the music for the *Losing It* visit www.ninalemon.com/plays

Downloadable versions are available from Salamander Street and are included within your performance licence fee.

Characters

POPPY

ROB

MADDIE

MIKE

CHARLOTTE

ASH

SEREN

TIM

SALLY

MELANIE

DAVID

LUCY

MAXINE

DANNO

CARYL

POLICE W

POLICE M

TIM'S MUM

POPPY'S DAD

KID 1

KID 2

KID 3

KID 4

KID 5

PROLOGUE

Year 13 enter. It is their last day of secondary school. Throughout the play the class will watch on as we flashback to various times during their previous seven years at secondary school. The class play their younger selves and also comment on the action with the benefit of their experience.

ROB: We are the class of 2019. *(Insert most recent school leavers' year.)*

POPPY: We have a shared history

DAVID: We share our stories

MELANIE: We overlap

SALLY: We coincide

SEREN: Where one story finishes

TIM: Another one starts.

ASH: We know each other's dark stuff

CHARLOTTE: The stuff we don't care to talk about

MELANIE: The people we cared about

POPPY: And I can't believe it's over

SALLY: And we're getting ready to say goodbye

MADDIE: Seven years at secondary school

ROB: Seven years to work it all out

POPPY: Some of us fell in love

SEREN: Some of us fell apart

CHARLOTTE: All of us changed

DAVID: None of us were quite the same as when we started

POPPY: As little kids in year 7

MIKE: Just eleven

MELANIE: Bags were bigger

SALLY: Skirts were longer

CHARLOTTE: Our minds got changed

MIKE: Voices got deeper

ROB: As our bodies grew taller

MADDIE: Not kids no more

SALLY: But young men and women

DAVID: And I keep thinking

POPPY: How did all this happen?

ROB: How did we get here?

MELANIE: Through first loves and/

ROB: And/ first times

CHARLOTTE: Innocent kisses

SEREN: And horrendous crimes

POPPY: But we survived.

TIM: The words we'll use, they're big and they're bold

ASH: So if you're easily offended you might want to close your eyes and ears

SEREN: 'Cause we will tell you the truth just how it happened. We're not going to clean it up

MADDIE: Or patronise you 'cause you've probably had enough of that already.

DAVID: 'Cause now most schools tell you how to put on a condom but, all that other stuff

SALLY: That's missed out

MIKE: And we're left trying to fill in the gaps.

MADDIE: This play is sex education with a difference.

ROB: We *are* the class of 2019.

POPPY: And this is our story.

SCENE 1

DAVID: Year 7.

POPPY: We are 11 years old.

ASH: The first year of big school and none of us have a clue.

POPPY: I feel grown up.

DAVID: I feel small.

ASH: I feel sick.

POPPY: The three of us knew each other from before.

ASH: So we stuck together.

DAVID: Helped each other out until…

A group of older kids barge past and the trio are separated. Four year 7 girls **MELANIE, SALLY, MADDIE** *and* **CHARLOTTE** *appear.*

MADDIE: Is he your boyfriend?

POPPY: What?

SALLY: Are you and him together?

POPPY: What? Err No way. Yuck.

MADDIE: Don't say it like that. I would.

MELANIE: Would ya?

SALLY: Yeah. Wouldn't you?

CHARLOTTE: Oh yeah, yeah. I totally would.

POPPY: You'd what?

MADDIE: He's cute

POPPY: What would you do?

MADDIE: I'm just saying I would and she would. We would.

POPPY: You would what?

MELANIE: What?

ASH: You keep saying I would, she would, we would. Well you would what?

MELANIE: There's no need to be like that about it.

ASH: Like what?

MADDIE: Maybe she fancies him?

ASH: I don't.

SALLY: Just as well 'cause I don't think he would with someone like you.

ASH: Thanks.

MADDIE: No offence. You're just not…

POPPY: What's she not?

SALLY: You know…

POPPY: Not really.

MELANIE: Look we're just saying we would with him but he wouldn't with her 'cause she's not…

ASH: Is anyone going to complete a sentence?

SALLY: Ssshh he's coming…

DAVID: Oh err hi.

The girls run away giggling.

DAVID: What was that about?

ASH: I literally have no idea.

DAVID: Girls are weird.

ASH: Yeah.

POPPY: No we're not.

DAVID: What's going on?

POPPY: Err nothing. Look, we should go.

ASH: What?

POPPY: We don't want them to think we would.

DAVID: Would what?

POPPY: *(To* **ASH**.*)* Come on!

Back in modern day.

POPPY: I was one of the innocent ones. People would say stuff like that and I'd have no idea what they meant.

SEREN: To be fair, you're still a bit like that.

POPPY: Oi.

ASH: I didn't want to know.

POPPY: I just went along with it so I didn't look stupid.

SEREN: Well that worked.

MADDIE: I didn't know either.

SALLY: Nor me.

DAVID: What? You were the one who started it.

MADDIE: I'd heard my mum say it about Phillip Schofield.

ASH: Wow.

POPPY: It was around then that things started to get complicated.

ASH: Yep.

DAVID: All of a sudden it was like a wall got built up. Boys on one side.

POPPY: Girls on the other.

DAVID: And we couldn't talk to each other

POPPY: Or listen to each other any more.

ASH: And if you didn't quite fit on one side or the other you were stuck with no place to be.

DAVID: If you're a boy, you're supposed to be into football

POPPY: And if you're a girl you're supposed to be into make up

ROB: And computer games

POPPY: And fashion

DAVID: And music

POPPY: And Snapchat

MIKE: And porn.

POPPY: What? That's disgusting. At 11?

MIKE: Yeah, so what?

ASH: It's a bit young mate.

MIKE: Not really. It was Rob who showed me first.

POPPY: Rob!

ROB: It was a long time ago.

MELANIE: Ha!

POPPY: You said you weren't into that stuff.

MADDIE: Trouble in paradise.

ROB: I'm not Pops really.

POPPY: You better not be.

ROB: We were just little kids.

MIKE: Are you kidding. The stuff you had on your phone bruv that was complete and utter filth.

ROB: It was before I knew you.

MIKE: Do you remember that video right with that Hungarian girl and she...

(**DAVID** *stops* **MIKE** *in his tracks.*)

ROB: I don't remember

MIKE: Ow! What was that for? So this girl. She had her hair in pigtails and she was all ooooooh....

(**ROB** *stops* **MIKE** *in his tracks.*)

ROB: Have I ever mentioned how beautiful your eyes are.

MIKE: Why does everyone keep doing that!

POPPY: Okay busted.

ASH: You have to tell us now.

ROB: What? Seriously? You don't want to...

MADDIE: I think we do.

MELANIE: Come on then.

POPPY: Spill.

ASH: Got to give the ladies what they want.

ROB: Really?

SALLY: *(To* **MIKE.***)* Pleeeaaasse!

MIKE: Alright!

SCENE 2

MIKE: So I'm in the playground with Tim and Dave and Rob comes over with his phone.

Back to year 7.

ROB: You are not going to believe this.

TIM: What is it?

ROB: Watch this.

MIKE: And he is pushing the phone screen right up in our faces and there's a girl there and it's summer so it's hot, and she's by a swimming pool so she's in a bikini and she's blonde.

SALLY: Of course she is.

MELANIE: What's that supposed to mean?

SALLY: They always are

POPPY: Shhh.

MIKE: And she's eating a ice lolly and she's licking it.
And then it jump cuts and her bikini just disappears.

MELANIE: Of course.

MADDIE: That happens to me all the time.

SALLY: Oh yep there go my knickers.

MADDIE: Whoopsie!

MIKE: And she's dripping the juice of the ice lolly down her body.

CHARLOTTE: Sounds sticky.

POPPY: Shut up!

MIKE: And she's sort of tracing the curves of her body with the lolly and the camera is working its way down there until it's right by her…and I guess I'm shocked but I like it. I hadn't really seen a girl like that before and Rob's almost wetting himself laughing and keeps saying…

ROB: Wait for it. Wait. You're gonna love this.

MIKE: And he's watching my face for a reaction and the girl on the screen she gets the ice lolly which is melting a lot now and she puts it down there.

LADS: Ooohhhhh.

POPPY: What?

CHARLOTTE: Why would you do that?

SEREN: How is that sexy?

SALLY: Why would anyone in their right mind want to put ice there?

MADDIE: It's got to hurt.

MELANIE: I don't know.

MIKE: And she's kind of showing off for the camera with the lolly...

ROB: Wait, wait you've got to see this.

MIKE: And she gets the lolly and sticks it back in her mouth.

LADS: Ewwwwww

DAVID: I know right. She is proper dirty.

MIKE: Yeah totally minging.

ROB: Do you wanna watch it again?

MIKE: Yeah alright.

Back to modern day.

MADDIE: If she's totally disgusting why would you watch it?

ROB: We were just stupid kids. We didn't know.

MELANIE: I don't get what's so gross about it any way. It's her body.

MIKE: Yeah but no self-respecting girl is going to do something like that on camera. It's gross.

SALLY: You're the ones watching it.

ROB: Not any more.

POPPY: So you're saying you don't look at it any more.

ROB: I've told you. No.

MADDIE: What about you?

DAVID: What?

MADDIE: Do you still watch it?

DAVID: Sometimes I have a look.

MELANIE: You do realise that what you're looking at is made up right?

MADDIE: It's not like that in real life.

DAVID: Yeah, I'm not stupid.

MADDIE: Good 'cause girls aren't all blonde with disappearing bikinis, no pubic hair and ice lollies on their bits.

SALLY: Bits really?

MADDIE: What? It's what my mum says.

SALLY: I just didn't know we were saying bits now.

MADDIE: What do you want me to say?

SALLY: Err how about vagina.

MADDIE: Eww.

SALLY: Oh sure. Bits isn't embarrassing but vagina is.

MIKE: Yeah, you wanna give that up mate.

ROB: Coming from you?

MIKE: What?

ROB: I may have been the first one to get hold of it but you're the grand daddy of it. I've never met anyone with a porn collection as big as yours. It's all you talked about.

MIKE: Yeah well things change.

DAVID: But you loved that stuff.

MIKE: Well I guess I grew up.

MADDIE: So you're not going to tell them the real reason you stopped it?

MIKE: You promised.

SALLY: No wonder you were such a crap boyfriend.

MIKE: Well thanks a lot.

SCENE 3

SALLY: So it's year 8 and Melanie won't stop going on about Tim.

SEREN: Tim?

MELANIE: Yeah. Sorry.

SEREN: I didn't know you'd been out with Tim.

MELANIE: It was only a few weeks.

SALLY: But in year 8 terms that means you're practically married.

MELANIE: So, I passed this note to Tim in history. It said will you go out with me?

SALLY: Cute.

MADDIE: Original.

MELANIE: And he sent a note back.

SEREN: What did it say?

MELANIE: Can Mike come?

CHARLOTTE: What?

MADDIE: That's a bit weird.

MELANIE: Well I realise that now but at the time.

We flashback to year 8 whilst the sixth form class looks on.

MELANIE: Sally. Will you double date with me?

SALLY: What? Who with?

MELANIE: Mike?

SALLY: Which one's Mike?

MELANIE: Over there.

SALLY: And I'm looking over at Mike and I'm thinking he looks…clean.

MADDIE: Clean?

SALLY: Yeah not grubby like some other guys.

MADDIE: I know what you mean but did you fancy him?

SALLY: Absolutely not.

CHARLOTTE: So why go out with him?

SALLY: Melanie wanted me to and she was doing these big puppy dog eyes.

MELANIE: Pleaasse.

SALLY: Okay. So before I know it some how Mel is going out with Tim and I'm paired up with Mike.

MADDIE: You and Mike. OMG. That's ridiculous.

CHARLOTTE: Did you actually physically go anywhere?

SALLY: Not much. We did go to the park a couple of times.

MELANIE: Don't remind me.

SCENE 4

Year 8.

MELANIE: Do I look alright?

SALLY: You look great.

MELANIE: Have I got lipstick on my teeth?

SALLY: No.

MELANIE: Smell my breath.

SALLY: What?

MELANIE: Smell me.

SALLY: Minty fresh.

MELANIE: Are you sure?

SALLY: Yes. Now will you just relax. Look here they are.

MIKE *and* **TIM** *arrive.* **MIKE** *has a football.* **MELANIE** *goes up to* **TIM** *and kisses him on the cheek.*

MIKE *slaps* **SALLY** *on the bum.*

MIKE: Alright babes.

SALLY: Hi.

From modern day.

MADDIE: I can't believe she didn't slap him back.

Back to the park.

SALLY: You're really late. We said eleven and it's almost twelve.

TIM: Sorry.

MIKE: Chill out. We were playing Xbox.

SALLY: Right.

From modern day.

CHARLOTTE: He'd kept her waiting, hadn't bothered texting and she let him get away with that?

Back to the park.

MELANIE: *(To* **TIM**.*)* So what do you want to do babes?

TIM: I don't know. What do you want to do?

At this point a girl jogs past and **MIKE**'*s eyes follow her.*

MIKE: *(Shouting after her.)* Hey baby. You want to be careful you don't knock yourself out!

Did you see the size of her…? *(Indicates breasts.)*

MIKE *starts messing with a football.*

MIKE: Wanna play?

TIM: *(To* **MEL**.*)* Do you mind?

MELANIE: Course not.

SALLY: Can we play?

MIKE: Yeah right. Girls don't play football. Sit on that bench.

Time passes. The girls look bored and intermittently reluctantly cheer for the boys.

MELANIE: Okay favourite book.

SALLY: No contest. Lord of the Rings.

MELANIE: You're kidding.

SALLY: No. I know it's a bit sad...

MELANIE: I love Lord of the Rings. I'm completely obsessed.

SALLY: How did I not know that?

MELANIE: Who's your favourite character?

SALLY: Legolas.

MELANIE: I love Legolas. "Shall I describe it to you...

BOTH: ...Or would you like me to get you a box!"

SALLY: Ooh have you heard the fools' theory?

MELANIE: No.

SALLY: Okay this is going to blow your mind!

MELANIE: Right. I'm ready.

SALLY: Gandalf always meant to use the eagles but didn't want to tell them otherwise it might leak out and he wanted the element of surprise so that's why the last thing he says to them is ..

MELANIE: Fly you fools.

SALLY: Exactly but they don't get it.

MELANIE: You're right, Mind totally blown.

> **MEL** *suddenly and unexpectedly starts doing a Gollum impression.*

MELANIE: Gollum gollum stupid little hobbitus.

> **SALLY** *laughs a lot.*

SALLY: You're brilliant.

SALLY has a go.

SALLY: My precious.

From modern day.

CHARLOTTE: They were so clearly perfect for each other.

Back to park.

MELANIE: That was rubbish.

The boys return.

MIKE: What's so funny?

The girls quickly compose themselves.

TIM: What are you talking about?

SALLY: Make up

MELANIE: *(At the same time.)* Hair.

MIKE: Typical. Right I'm bored. Wanna play truth or dare?

SALLY: I don't know.

MIKE: You're not scared are you?

SALLY: No way.

MIKE: Okay, I'll start.

> **MIKE** *pulls* **SALLY** *onto his lap and holds her tight she smiles nervously.* **MELANIE** *sits on* **TIM***'s lap.*

MIKE: Tim. Truth or dare.

TIM: Truth.

MIKE: Who do you think the fittest girl in the year is?

TIM: I don't want to say.

MIKE: Them's the rules mate.

TIM: I'm shy.

MELANIE: It's okay. I won't mind.

TIM: Okay. It is you though.

MELANIE: Ooh I'm flattered.

MIKE: Okay and follow up question. What the best bit of her?

MELANIE: Mike!

TIM: I really like your eyes. They're pretty and I like the way you look at me.

MELANIE: Aaaah.

MIKE: Bleurgh. Pass me a bucket.

SALLY: Oi!

MIKE: Okay. So it's your turn.

TIM: Erm. Ok Mike. Truth or dare?

MIKE: Truth.

TIM: Err. Who do you think the hottest girl in the year is?

MIKE: Good question. Unoriginal but good. Now let's see errr…
I think Poppy's got the best bum…but I'd want Melanie's legs…

MELANIE: Thanks?

MIKE: But it's got to be Maddie up top *(indicates breasts)* And…

TIM: What about her face?

MIKE: Haven't really thought about it but maybe Charlotte's yeah she's got serious 'come to bed' eyes…and I wouldn't kick her out of bed…

MELANIE: What about Sally?

SALLY: Don't worry about it.

MIKE: Oh don't get all silly about it. I'm here with you aren't I and I mean you're easily like up there in the top twenty percent of my list.

MELANIE: You've got a list?

MIKE: Yeah.

MELANIE: But you're meant to be going out with Sally.

MIKE: So?

SALLY: Leave it Mel. It doesn't matter.

MIKE: Are you upset?

SALLY: No.

MIKE: Your face has all gone red.

SALLY: I'm just hot.

MIKE: That's well funny.

MELANIE: What's wrong with you?

MIKE: What?

MELANIE: You can't say that in front of her. You're supposed to be going out.

MIKE: I'm just being honest aren't I?

MELANIE: You're being nasty.

SALLY: Leave it.

MELANIE: No. I won't. How dare you!

MIKE: No need to have a strop. Time of the month is it?

MELANIE: No. You're just some kind of idiot who thinks that girls only matter for what they look like and how big their breasts are. But she's funny and intelligent and kind and one of the prettiest girls in the year and basically way too good for you! Come on, we're going.

Tim?

TIM *for a moment looks torn between his friend and girlfriend.*

TIM: Err.

MIKE: Are you gonna let your girlfriend talk to me like that? Stupid cow.

TIM: Erm.

MELANIE: Okay. I'm going to make this really easy for you. Tim, you're dumped.

TIM: What did I do?

MELANIE: Come on Sal.

They walk off.

MIKE: *(Shouting after* **SAL.***)* I'll text you.

SALLY: *(Shouting back.)* You're dumped too.

MIKE: I didn't fancy you anyway.

Back to modern day.

MIKE: Yeah I mean it all makes sense now that you two…

MELANIE: That's got nothing to do with it. You were just being a total idiot.

MADDIE: Yep, why break a habit of a lifetime eh?

SALLY: We didn't have the first clue about relationships. I didn't know what to expect.

MELANIE: It's not like anyone ever talked to us about that stuff.

SCENE 5

MADDIE: They did a bit. In year 8, we had that whole day where all we did was sex education.

MELANIE: Did we?

MIKE: I don't remember.

LUCY: I think I was off that day.

ASH: Yeah. How can you forget? They had these visitors come into the school.

DANNO: Hi. I'm Danno. You can call me Danno.

MAXINE: And I'm Maxine. You can call me Maxine.

MIKE: They got out all these pretend penises.

POPPY: Demonstrators.

SALLY: Dildos.

ASH: And we had to practice putting a condom on.

DANNO: Hey guys. Yeah let's all settle down because today we're going to be learning about, oh yes, I've said it…

DANNO AND MAXINE: Sex!

POPPY: Totally cringe.

MIKE: Miss. What's your favourite position Miss?

MAXINE: We're not talking about positions thank you very much.

DANNO: So if everyone can take a demonstrator.

MAXINE: It's one between two.

SALLY: That's heteronormative Miss.

DANNO: For demonstrating purposes there's one demonstrator between two.

(The class mess around.)

MADDIE: Hey Poppy. I'm a unicorn.

POPPY: Dickhead.

MIKE: Don't they come in different colours?

SALLY: That's well racist.

ASH: They do come in different colours.

DANNO: So if everyone takes a condom.

MIKE: What if it's not big enough?

DANNO: One size fits all.

ROB: That's what they told you.

They mess around. **MELANIE** *takes* **ROB***'s demonstrator and starts joking around with* **SALLY**.

MIKE: Maxine, I can't find my penis. Maxine, my penis has gone missing. Can you help me find it?

MAXINE: I'll help you in a minute.

ALL: Ooohhhhhh!

MAXINE: Right so if each pair take a condom. So first you have to check it's not out of date.

SALLY: And they are going through the whole thing about how to put on a condom properly but I'm tuning out. Somehow I know this is not going to be relevant for me…

DANNO: And then check for the little heart shaped symbol or CE sign. That's the kite mark and means it's safe to use.

SALLY: And I'm looking at Melanie and she's laughing and she looks so beautiful when she smiles so I'm smiling too…

MAXINE: Open the packet making sure to keep the roll on the outside so it looks like a Mexican hat.

SALLY: And she's wearing the condom on her head now and we're messing around and my tummy is turning over and my heart is beating and my hands are sweating and I think I'm falling in love with her.

DANNO: And then you hold it with one hand squeezing the tip ensuring there's no air trapped in there…

SALLY: And it's not like some big revelation or lightning bolt. I never really had a crush on a boy and I was just waiting for it to come because everybody made out it would happen. But for me it didn't happen and I'm ok with that.

MAXINE: And roll the condom down the shaft.

SALLY: And the way they went on in sex education class you'd think that everyone was straight and the only time we'd get mentioned is when boys are watching porn or some girls get off with each other for attention but that's not what it was for me. I'm just a girl who liked girls, well this particular girl, and I'm okay with that.

We are back in the modern day.

MELANIE: You never told me that before.

SALLY: You never asked.

MELANIE: You're so cute. *(She kisses her shoulder.)*

SALLY: Stop it.

ROB: But you two weren't together back then?

SALLY: Nope. I never thought she'd be into me.

MELANIE: Why not?

SALLY: All you ever did was talk about boys.

MELANIE: So.

SALLY: So you're seriously telling me that if thirteen-year-old me had asked out thirteen year old you then you'd have been up for it.

MELANIE: Maybe not. But I'd have been an idiot for turning you down.

SALLY: Ahh.

MIKE: So were you lying about being into those guys.

MELANIE: Not really.

MIKE: But you guys are together now?

SALLY: Well durr.

MIKE: What? Surely you either like one or the other?

SALLY: Just 'cause you're insecure about your sexuality doesn't mean…

MIKE: I am not insecure. I've had the sex with loads of girls.

MELANIE: Like who.

MIKE: You don't know them. They're not from around here.

MADDIE: Ha!

MIKE: So come on. What is it. Boys or girls?

MELANIE: Oh Michael. You have so much to learn.

SALLY: People don't all fit into your little boxes.

　　MAXINE *and* **DANNO** *appear.*

DANNO: That's right.

MAXINE: People can be all the colours of the rainbow.

DAVID: Where did they come from?

MELANIE: Maybe someone needs a bit more sex education.

DANNO: Hit it.

Song – A to Z Sexuality

MAXINE: Let's start at the very beginning
It's a very good place to start
When you're young you'd have learned your ABCs
Now it's time to be concerned with LG and B.

ASH: What about T?

MAXINE: With our handy A to Z of sexuality.

SALLY: A's for asexual, that's someone who doesn't feel sexual desire.

MELANIE: B is bisexual people who're into both women and men.

SALLY: You see now, you're on fire.

BOTH: C's for consenting adults,
Yes you must make sure that they agree
Whatever sexuality
And D is for desire,
When you feel a fire
In your heart and your mind

ALL: We've made a little A to Z

30

So understanding becomes easy
There's something special about being alphabetical when there's so much to learn

MIKE: E, F, G is for gay, like men who love men and for women the same

DANNO: You've got it.

SALLY: H I J K L is lesbian, a special word for women who are exclusively gay.

MAXINE: M N O is for orgasm that's the moment when
Some people shout out
Or some flail about

DANNO: P is pansexual, which is someone who could be attracted to anyone

MAXINE: And Qs for queer or questioning 'cause R is that it's reasonable to love anyone you like

ALL: Oh we've made a little A to Z
So understanding becomes easy
There's something special about being alphabetical when there's so much to learn

MAXINE: S stands for sex – in the eyes of the law
You should wait till you're sixteen
And maybe even more

DANNO: T is for teenager

ASH: Is this some sort of joke?

DANNO: 'Cause your bodies are changing
and your voices are broke.

DANNO and MAXINE Kids think that they are mature
But they are just really insecure
And should wait till they're sure

MAXINE: 'Cause the thing you need to learn
And you'll learn to accept

Is that most kids are sixteen
Before they've had sex!

ALL: What?
We've made a little A to Z
So understanding becomes easy
There's something special about being alphabetical when there's so much
to learn

MIKE: U know if you are gay?
Does that mean you fancy me bruv?

DANNO: Do you think all straight girls do
Don't fancy yourself luv!

MIKE: *(To* **MELANIE** *and* **SALLY***.)* You know when you two are doing it
Is there any chance of viewing it?

MELANIE and SAL: Urrgh no!

MAXINE: Very many people think that lesbian sex is a spectator's sport.
That's another untruth brought to you mainly from watching porn.
W-ell don't ask if you can watch,
Put an X in that silly question box
Y don't you remember that kindness is key
CoZ you're more likely to be bullied if you're LG or B

ASH: Or T!

ALL: We've made a little A to Z
So understanding becomes easy
There's something special about being alphabetical when there's so much
to learn
And there's so much to learn

POPPY: Okay. We definitely didn't cover half that stuff.

CHARLOTTE: It's like people thought we were too young.

ROB: Well year 8…we were just kids

CHARLOTTE: Yeah but they couldn't keep us like that for ever.
    We lived in the real world and sex….sex is everywhere!

ROB: What do you mean?

SCENE 6

CHARLOTTE: Okay. So year 8. I'm on the bus. Two lads get on and take the seats in front. It's busy. It's summer. It's hot.

She removes her hoodie.

No air. Old people. Frazzled mums with screaming toddlers. School kids. Me.

All crushed up together. It's hard to breathe. Someone at some point has eaten a KFC and I can smell rotting chicken which is just finished off by a slight pong from one of the whingeing toddlers' bums. Nice.

I'm looking out the window and I catch a glimpse of something in the window. It's the light of the screen on the phone of the guy in front and it draws my eye.

It's a video. A girl. She only looks about my age and she's completely naked. She seems unsteady and her eyes look unfocused. Like she's taken something.

I can't hear the sound but she looks like she's talking to someone behind the camera or listening to instructions because she starts to touch herself and twist about. She looks weird and cold and just very, very sad.

Suddenly I feel really aware of my vest top and my body.

She pulls her hoodie back on.

She's the one who's naked but I feel exposed. And there's men now in the video too.

Three men appear and they start to do things to her or make her do things to them. She doesn't know what's happening and the men are laughing.

I don't want to see that. I want to look away. I want to pretend I never saw it in the first place but something is stopping me and I can't stop looking and she's on the bed now and the men surround her.

And I wonder if that's what it's supposed to be like, if that's what boys really want and it's in close up now and you can see everything and her skin's got these goose bumps. She's not really there anymore and her eyes roll back into her head and she just flesh now not a person at all but they don't seem to care and the video keeps going and I keep watching. And then suddenly I realise all at once and too late that the lads with the phone are staring straight at me. And I wasn't watching the reflection in the end. I was staring straight at the phone screen through the gap in the seats and they've seen me and they're smirking at me and I feel afraid and pathetic and tiny and ashamed. I feel my face flush red. And the guy with the phone, he turns the screen round so it's right in front of my face. And they're laughing at me and, as they head for the doors, his mate leans in so close I can smell him and whispers 'pervert' before jumping off the bus.

And I see them laughing and pointing as they skip down the road. I'm sure everyone on the bus has seen what happened so I put my head down and wait for my stop. Maybe they're right. Maybe I am a pervert or something. Why did I want to look? I'm not a lesbian. And my heart is still beating fast whilst I walk home from the bus and I'm angry with myself for not standing up for myself and I don't talk to anyone about it 'cause I don't want anyone to know.

We are back in modern day.

ROB: That's really horrible.

CHARLOTTE: I just wish I'd known what to say and I had no one to talk to about it. I actually felt dirty.

ROB: Why on earth were they watching it on a bus? What creeps.

SALLY: Why are you surprised? Things like that happen all the time.

ROB: What? No they don't.

SALLY: Not to you but they do to us. Stuff that makes you feel scared.

MELANIE: Like you can't walk anywhere without blokes shouting stuff…

MADDIE: And you get so many pictures of willies that you actually get too bored to be shocked.

SALLY: Willies?

MADDIE: What?

SALLY: Nothing – I just didn't get the willy memo.

MADDIE: I'm just trying to keep things appropriate.

SALLY: So willy is appropriate but penis…

MADDIE: I hate that word.

ROB: What wrong with penis?

POPPY: When I was little I thought it was pronounced pen-is.

MELANIE: Oh bless.

POPPY: I'd only seen it written down.

MADDIE: It just makes me feel weird.

SALLY: Peeeeenis.

MELANIE: Penis.

MADDIE: Will you quit it.

SALLY: Penis penis penis.

MADDIE: Stop it.

CHARLOTTE: So the whole thing just made me feel really uncomfortable.

ROB: I'm not surprised. That's disgusting.

CHARLOTTE: Yeah I know. What if some little kid had seen it?

ROB: Charlotte, you were a little kid.

POPPY: You're lovely.

ROB: Thank you.

They snuggle.

MADDIE: Can you guys get a room?

They keep cuddling.

MADDIE: Not all of us get to find our soul mate you know.
No need to rub it in.

They continue cuddling.

SCENE 7

MADDIE: So we're in year 9 and I'm just scrolling through my messages when Charlotte rocks up.

MADDIE is scrolling through images on her phone.

MADDIE: Willy. Willy. Oh hang on. Nope another willy.

CHARLOTTE: What you doing?

MADDIE: Just catching up on my admin.

CHARLOTTE: What?

She shows her the phone screen.

CHARLOTTE: Euurgh! That's gross.

MADDIE: I know right. They just keep on coming.

Cut to modern day.

MELANIE: Unfortunate turn of phrase.

SALLY *giggles and we jump back to year 9.*

CHARLOTTE: Why do you think they do it?

MADDIE: What?

CHARLOTTE: Send us pictures of their…you know..

MADDIE: Beats me babe.

CHARLOTTE: Do you think any girls actually get turned on by that?

MADDIE: I dunno. Not me babes. Don't get me wrong I like boys but I prefer kind of whole boys rather than just some dissected bit of them. It's well weird. Look at this one?

CHARLOTTE: Urrrghh I didn't realise they could be so bendy.

MADDIE: All shapes and sizes innit mate.

CHARLOTTE: What do you think they're hoping to achieve?

MADDIE: They want a pic back innit.

CHARLOTTE: You're not sending them pics are you?

MADDIE: What do you think I am babes? An idiot? It's illegal to do it if you're under 18 and you can't trust those guys with something like that. No way.

CHARLOTTE: Good. If I tell you something do you absolutely promise that you won't tell anyone anything ever about it.

MADDIE: OMG. Cross my heart and hope to die I will never tell a lie. Pinky promise babe.

CHARLOTTE: I met someone.

MADDIE: Ahhh! I can't believe it. So tell me everything and I mean everything!

CHARLOTTE: Alright. So his name's Malcolm.

MADDIE: Malcolm?

CHARLOTTE: What? I think it's cute.

MADDIE: Yeah, yeah, sorry babes. How long's this been going on?

CHARLOTTE: A few weeks.

MADDIE: Why didn't you tell me babes? We're meant to be besties.

CHARLOTTE: I didn't know if it was going anywhere.

MADDIE: So what's he like?

CHARLOTTE: Well he's got dark hair.

MADDIE: I love dark hair.

CHARLOTTE: And blue eyes.

MADDIE: Oh wow blue eyes and dark hair is like my all time favourite combination on a boy. Actually blue eyes are my total favourite ever after brown and hazel but other than that they're my favourite.

CHARLOTTE: Right.

MADDIE: Is he tall?

CHARLOTTE: He's tallish.

MADDIE: That's good babes. You don't want to get neck injury reaching up to kiss him.

CHARLOTTE: No.

MADDIE: Is he a good kisser? Are you guys going out or are you just seeing each other.

CHARLOTTE: We're just seeing where it goes.

MADDIE: Cool. Cool.

CHARLOTTE: I haven't kissed him yet.

MADDIE: Taking your time. I like that. So when can I meet him?

CHARLOTTE: The thing is, and this is the really annoying part, he lives a really long way away.

MADDIE: Oh my God. Long distance. That's super romantic. You're like Romeo and Juliet except they ended up dead babes and you don't want that. So how did you meet him? Was it at your cousin's wedding? You looked well hot in that dress. If I was a lesbian, which I totally am not, not that there's anything wrong with that or nothing, but it's not really for me, I mean I like girls as friends but I'm not romantically inclined that way, but if I was I would with you in that dress if you know what I mean.

CHARLOTTE: Erm thanks? It wasn't at the wedding. He liked one of my instagram posts and we just got talking.

MADDIE: He's a randomer?

CHARLOTTE: Well he was but we talked and got to know each other. He's really intelligent and I can just talk to him about anything you know?

MADDIE: But you have met him in real life too?

CHARLOTTE: Not yet.

MADDIE: Babes that's really exciting. When are you going to meet him face to face? Oooh do you think you'll run into his arms and he'll scoop you up and swing you around and then take you for McDonald's?

CHARLOTTE: Err I doubt it. He's a vegan.

MADDIE: Like you babes. You're both veggie together. That's so sweet.

CHARLOTTE: We've got loads in common. We like the same books, TV, and get this, he even watches wildlife documentaries.

MADDIE: Oh mate. You is all over those animal programs.

CHARLOTTE: I know. His favourite animal's a koala bear

MADDIE: Oh oh oh! And yours is the Kangaroo

CHARLOTTE: *(Overlapping.)* Kangaroo. I know what are the chances?

MADDIE: You're like meant to be together. You hopping about and him hugging some tree and eating bamboo.

CHARLOTTE: Isn't that Pandas?

MADDIE: I don't care. You're like marsupial mates. So when are you meeting up?

CHARLOTTE: I'm not sure. He's pretty busy.

MADDIE: Has he got exams?

CHARLOTTE: No. He's not at school.

MADDIE: College guy!

CHARLOTTE: He's finished college.

MADDIE: How old is he?

CHARLOTTE: Twenty.

MADDIE: That's a bit old mate.

CHARLOTTE: Yeah, I know but we just clicked and you can't control who you click with.

MADDIE: Sure, sure, but isn't it a bit weird?

CHARLOTTE: No. He said in my picture I looked at least 16.

MADDIE: That's right babes. You totally do. You is well mature.

CHARLOTTE: That's what he said.

MADDIE: Is he like asking you to send pics?

CHARLOTTE: No.

MADDIE: That's all boys round here want these days. Send us a pic. Send us a pic.

CHARLOTTE: He's not like that.

MADDIE: Does he write stuff to you that's proper dirty?

CHARLOTTE: No. He says he wants to get to know me first.

MADDIE: Isn't it like illegal?

CHARLOTTE: I can talk to who I like. There's no law against talking.

MADDIE: Course babes. Just a bit of a big age difference that's all.

CHARLOTTE: Yeah but like Malcolm says. It seems big now but when we're like 30 and 37 no one will think anything about it.

MADDIE: Yeah, when you put it like that they're just being ageist innit.

CHARLOTTE: I really like him. He's not like other guys. He even wants to get to know my friends.

MADDIE: Yeah you got to introduce me so he can set me up with one of his mates. I'm sick of the boys around here.

SCENE 8

Back in the modern day.

DAVID: I used to hear that a lot.

MADDIE: What?

DAVID: Boys are all rubbish. Boys only want one thing.

CHARLOTTE: Well don't you?

MIKE: No. Some of us have a sensitive side you know.

MADDIE: You obviously just hide it really well.

ASH: He's right though. We're not exactly portrayed in the most flattering light.

ROB: Everyone thinks boys have to want sex and that we're so shallow that's all that matters.

ASH: Well not all guys are like that.

SCENE 9

ASH: So. It's year 9 and we're all stressing out about options but they still found time to do the one day thing again only this time we talked about relationships too.

MIKE: Did we?

ASH: Yeah.

LUCY: I think I was off that day.

ASH: And the same people came in again.

DANNO: Hi guys. I'm Danno. Dan the man.

ROB: Oh God.

POPPY: I liked him.

MADDIE: You would.

MAXINE: And I'm Maxine.

MIKE: She was well fit.

ASH: Not really the point.

SALLY: She was though.

MELANIE: Oi!

DANNO: Okay guys. Let's talk about relationships and, oh yes I've said it, let's talk about the sex.

SEREN: Cringe.

MAXINE: So we're going to split into two groups. Boys over there with Danno and girls over there with me. Go!

MELANIE: Tash, Natasha!

ASH: What?

MELANIE: Girls over here!

ASH: Of course everyone assumed I was a girl. Even I sort of assumed it. So I'm sitting there with all the girls and we're being asked to write a list of all the qualities we'd be looking for in our perfect partner.

POPPY: He's got to be kind.

ROB: She's got to be intelligent.

MELANIE: Yeah and have a good sense of humour.

SALLY: Yeah.

SEREN: You've got to find him attractive physically.

TIM: You've got to have shared interests.

ASH: And they're going on about what they'd look for in a partner

CHARLOTTE: And he's got to have a really good jumper collection.

SEREN: What?

CHARLOTTE: You know so you can borrow his cosy jumpers.

MAXINE: I think we might be straying from the point slightly.

ASH: I'm tuning out. I don't feel comfortable here. I don't fit. Then, out of nowhere Sally says…

SALLY: We're sort of assuming that everyone wants a male partner but not all of us do.

ASH: She just came out and no one's really reacting.

SALLY: And my heart is thumping and I'm sure my face is all red because I just said it out loud and everyone is staring at me.

ASH: And I can't look at Sally. I'm sure she wants me to say that I'm the same as she is but I'm not the same.

MAXINE: Okay, so what qualities would you look for in a girl?

SALLY: And I'm talking about having someone I trust and can have a laugh with..

MELANIE: I can't believe Sally just came out and said it. It's not a big deal and I'd guessed anyway but to just come right out with it. She is so brave.

ASH: And whilst everyone's distracted by Sally's revelation, I'm straining my ears to hear what the boys are saying. And I can't quite make it out. I was expecting them to have some crude list. Skinny with big boobs and long legs. But their list don't look that different from ours. And without thinking about it I'm standing up and I'm wandering over to them.

MELANIE: Where are you going?

ASH: And somehow I've moved over to the boys and it feels good to be here in a way but then they're all looking at me and …

MIKE: Err can we help you?

ROB: Are you one of the lads now or what?

ASH: I'm just going to the loo.

MIKE: Gents is that way!

ASH: And I'm running out of the classroom and I'm locking myself in the disabled loo. I don't want to see anyone. And I feel more alone than I have ever felt in my life.

We're back to modern day.

SALLY: Sorry.

ROB: Yeah. We didn't know.

ASH: I didn't really know. I had to look it up online. No one had ever mentioned being trans before.

MIKE: Yeah, but, not being rude or anything but are you are boy or a girl 'cause I'm confused.

MELANIE: Are you really that stupid?

MIKE: What? I just don't understand. What is it? 'Cause I dunno how to be with it…

SALLY: You really are an idiot. *He's* a guy. Male pronouns. Different name.

MIKE: Yeah, but does that mean …you know down…

ASH: Why does it always come down to that?

    DANNO *and* **MAXINE** *appear.*

MAXINE: He's right.

MIKE: This is getting ridiculous.

DANNO: Hey buddy. It's not cool to ask about what's in people's pants.

MIKE: Haven't we got a right to know?

DANNO: It really is none of your business.

TRANSGENDER 101

ASH: Where gender is concerned
It's a little bit absurd
So many say that's it
You're a boy, or a girl
But the truth as you will see
Is it's more complex for me
A boy A girl
I just want you to see me

CHORUS: Why don't you tell them about the times
You've sat alone and cried?

ASH: Well I never felt I'd fit in
No matter what I tried
With the girls I felt alone
So I want to take hormones
I was ready for change
I even changed my name

CHORUS: So Ash is what he chose

A boy's name, and boys' clothes
The bullies think it's a joke
Oh Ash don't give up hope

ASH: It's so hard to explain
If you're a girl in your body and a boy in your brain
But sometimes it's harder if you don't feel like you're either
My friend is gender neutral and doesn't feel they fit anywhere
You cannot see a whole person by the length of their hair

CHORUS: There's trans and there is gay
But not both are the same
Some are and some are not
Some are bi and some are straight
We want to help you explain
Because you're not alone
There are laws in place to protect you
Oh Ash, don't give up hope

ASH: I don't to be bullied
I don't want to be scared
I don't want to be afraid of going anywhere
Just see me as a person
Judge me by my heart
A world of understanding
Just needs one person to start.

SCENE 10

POPPY: Why didn't you say anything?

ASH: I didn't know what to say. So I hung out with the girls and people generally accepted me. Charlotte even added me to this group chat she'd set up.

MADDIE: And Charlotte's introduced me to this guy Eddie online. He's amazing. And he's asking me questions and he really wants to get to know me as a person.

CHARLOTTE: And Mal's saying that, when things calm down at work, we should meet up. We can double date with Mads and Eddie and they'll transfer us some cash for the train.

ASH: And I'm scrolling through it and I can't really follow what's going on but everyone seems to be posting selfies and Maddie's posted this really pretty picture. And someone's typing. It's this guy Eddie.
'Wow. You are so beautiful. I just want to take care of you. One day I will marry you.'
And I'm thinking, that's a bit full on mate so, when I see my form tutor, I ask her about it. And she looks really worried and, before I know where I am, we're sitting in front of the deputy head and he's looking really serious and asking loads of questions.

SCENE 11

MADDIE: You are nothing more than a selfish, bitter little cow!

ASH: What?

MADDIE: Why would you do something like that?

ASH: I was worried.

MADDIE: If you were worried you should have talked to us about it not go blabbing to Mr. Simpson.

ASH: I'm sorry.

MADDIE: It's like because you're miserable you think everyone else should be. Thanks to you, Charlotte might not be able to speak to Mal ever again. You might not understand this but they actually love each other.

ASH: I'm sorry.

MADDIE: Teachers and God knows who else have been looking through our private messages. It's humiliating and you've done that. Her mum's been crying and you know what she's like at the best of times. They've called the police Ash. She's doesn't understand things like this. She won't be able to cope with this.

ASH: Where's Charlotte? I'll go and say sorry.

MADDIE: She's gone to sort things out.

ASH: What do you mean? Where is she?

MADDIE: Mind your own business.

ASH: Maddie. Where has she gone?

MADDIE: If you must know she's meeting up with Mal to say goodbye.

ASH: What?

MADDIE: Are you going to mess up that for her too?

ASH: Where is she meeting him?

MADDIE: The bus station. Get off me.

ASH runs off.

SCENE 12

CHARLOTTE: So I'm heading to the bus station and I'm hoping that I can find him. He's parking around the back so no one sees us. I'm falling in love and nothing has felt more right in my whole life.

ASH: So I'm running to the bus station and I'm hoping I can catch her. And I'm thinking something seems very, very wrong about this.

Back to modern day.

ROB: I can't believe he went after her on his own.

POPPY: That was a seriously dangerous plan.

ROB: He definitely should have told someone. They both could have been hurt.

POPPY: Yeah but you can't always think straight when something like that's happening.

Back to past.

ASH: And as I'm running I'm thinking what am I doing? I should have told someone. What if I'm wrong and this is some great love story and then I spot her...she's a little way ahead.

Charlotte! Wait! Charlotte.

CHARLOTTE: What do you want?

ASH: I just want to talk to you. That's all. Can we just talk?

CHARLOTTE: I'm busy. I've got to meet someone.

ASH: Yeah, I know who you're meeting.

CHARLOTTE: Why do you hate us?

ASH: I don't hate you.

CHARLOTTE: Then leave us alone.

ASH: I'm just not sure that he's who you think he is ok.

CHARLOTTE: What?

ASH: How much do you actually know about him?

CHARLOTTE: We've been talking every night for months so quite a lot actually. He really likes me.

ASH: What accent's he got.

CHARLOTTE: What kind of a question is that?

ASH: You said you'd talked loads and that he lived far away so I just thought he might have a cool accent.

CHARLOTTE: He just sounds normal okay?

ASH: You haven't heard his voice have you?

CHARLOTTE: He's shy. Look I think I know my own boyfriend.

ASH: Okay, what's he into?

CHARLOTTE: Not that this is anything to do with you but he likes cooking vegan food, animal conservation, campaigning to protect endangered species…

ASH: So all the things you're into…

CHARLOTTE: We've got a lot in common.

ASH: And all the stuff you're always posting online about?

CHARLOTTE: What?

ASH: Just saying it's a bit convenient. What do you actually know about him?

CHARLOTTE: I know enough.

ASH: Yeah, and I know enough to know that I don't think you should meet him alone so I'm coming with you.

CHARLOTTE: You're not.

ASH: Let's go.

Back to modern day.

POPPY: That's not a good idea. Now he's just leading them both into trouble.

Back to past.

CHARLOTTE: So I'm trying to meet Mal but Ash won't quit bugging me and I'm looking at my watch and not wanting to be late so I stop trying to argue and let her follow me.

ASH: And Charlotte's storming off and I'm following her as we cut down a side alley when I hear something behind me.

CHARLOTTE: And I glance over my shoulder and there's a group of kids between me and Ash and I can't make out what they're saying but…

ASH: They seem to come out of nowhere. Older kids and they get right up in my face. Excuse me.

KID 1: Are you a boy or a girl?

ASH: I need to get to my friend.

KID 1: 'Cause I can't work it out.

ASH: Can I get by?

KID 2: Maybe we need to check.

CHARLOTTE: And something doesn't look right but I don't want to miss Mal. Maybe they're friends of hers so I turn to go when I hear her cry out and I spin back round and I can see that they've got her up against the wall and I don't know what to do.

ASH: And they're holding my arms against the wall and I'm struggling but they're too strong.

CHARLOTTE: And I'm frozen to the spot and I look up and down but I can't see anyone.

ASH: And some girl's got this lipstick and they're forcing it onto my face.

KID 3: That's much better.

CHARLOTTE: And I can just see one of them start pulling at her trousers, trying to take them down and suddenly I'm forgetting about Malcolm and I'm really angry. I'm angry about every obscene photo, every lewd comment and all the boys who thought our bodies were theirs to mess around with.

ASH: And I hear Charlotte shout.

CHARLOTTE: GET OFF HER!
And it's flight or fight and I've chosen fight.
And I'm running towards them.

ASH: And it's almost funny as tiny little Charlotte comes racing to save me and she kind of catches them off guard and they laugh and one of them lunges for her and she screams.
And I mean proper, horror film style, ear piercing screaming.

CHARLOTTE: And it feels great.

ASH: And she doesn't stop screaming and I hear footsteps.

OFF STAGE: Oi. What's going on?

ASH: And I'm being punched in the stomach and thrown to the floor.

CHARLOTTE: And suddenly people are hearing me and wondering what's happening and those people who had Ash, they turn and *they* run away from *me*.

Both **ASH** *and* **CHARLOTTE** *are crying.*

CHARLOTTE: And I'm looking at Ash in a crumpled heap on the floor and it's like all this stuff with Mal's just not important. And I'm calling the police.

Back to modern day.

POPPY: That's horrible.

ROB: What happened next?

ASH: Charlotte stayed with me and made a statement to the police.

CHARLOTTE: I just didn't want those scum bags to get away with it.

DAVID: Were the police weird about it?

ASH: No. Actually they were brilliant. They really took me seriously.

ROB: Did they catch them?

ASH: No. It all happened so fast. We couldn't give them much to go on.

DAVID: Thank God Charlotte was there.

ASH: Yeah.

SALLY: What happened to Mal?

MELANIE: How did you miss this?

SALLY: I dunno.

CHARLOTTE: It turned out Malcolm wasn't who I thought he was.

MADDIE: None of them were. They were all in their fifties. Eddie *(that's not his real name)* was a known sex offender who was not long out of prison for raping two girls younger than us.

SALLY: Wow.

CHARLOTTE: It actually went to court. Turns out they were saying all that stuff to other groups of girls too.

ROB: So you were pretty lucky that Ash went after you.

CHARLOTTE: Yeah we know. He might have saved my life.

MADDIE: I have said sorry a lot of times.

ASH: Don't worry about it.

SCENE 13

POPPY: So year 9 was pretty rough all round. Roll on year 10.

ROB: Yeah with additional homework and extra stress.

POPPY: Some good things happened.

ROB: Really what was that?

She playfully shoves him.

POPPY: So I'm on a date with Rob. We're meeting up for a coffee.

ROB: Which we thought was the height of sophistication.

POPPY: And I haven't really been on a date before

ROB: And I haven't really liked anyone before

POPPY: So it's pretty awkward.

Silence. Then both go to speak at the same time.

ROB: Sorry.

POPPY: You go first.

ROB: No. Ladies first.

POPPY: I was just going to say did you hear about Sally and Melanie?

ROB: No.

POPPY: Sally asked Melanie out and she said yes.

ROB: Oh, I thought they were together already.

POPPY: No. Not officially.

ROB: Oh right. That's cool. Good for them.

POPPY: Yep.

Silence.

ROB: I was going to say.

POPPY: Yeah.

ROB: I really like your hair like that.

POPPY: Oh my God. It's a total disaster. It got really frizzy so I went to have it cut and now it looks awful.

ROB: And I'm thinking why can't she just take a compliment for once. I like it.

POPPY: Thanks.
And I'm thinking quick say something nice back. Compliment him. *(Pause.)*
I like your T shirt…?

ROB: It's a black T shirt.

POPPY: Yeah but it looks good on you. Oh God. I'm really bad at this.

ROB: You're not.

POPPY: I'm making a complete idiot of myself.

ROB: You're not. Just maybe…

POPPY: What?

ROB: Try and relax a bit.

POPPY: Okay.
And I'm thinking why am I being like this? I've known him since I was 11 and we've hung out literally loads of time but suddenly 'cause it's a date it feels different.

They drink their coffees. **ROB** *gets cream on his nose.* **POPPY** *giggles.*

ROB: What?

POPPY: Nothing.

ROB: Come on what?

POPPY: Here.

She leans in and takes the cream off his nose with her finger than eats it a little flirtatiously.

ROB: Smooth Rob. Really smooth.

But that's broken the ice and before long we're talking and it's not awkward anymore.

POPPY: And I love talking to him. I could talk to him for hours.

ROB: And suddenly time is leaping forward

POPPY: And it's so easy to be myself with him.

ROB: And I'm offering to walk her home

POPPY: And he's holding my hand when…

Message sound.

POPPY: Sorry. Hang on.

She checks her phone and **ROB** *awkwardly has to let go of her hand.*

ROB: Everything okay?

POPPY: Yeah, it's just this cat video that Maddie's tagged me in.

She shows him the video. He is not amused. They rejoin hands and walk. The phone goes again.

POPPY: Sorry. In case it's my mum…

They let go again.

POPPY: It's not. It's another video. Look.

Again he is unimpressed. They rejoin hands and walk. The phone goes again.

POPPY: Just leave it.

ROB: Cats can wait.

POPPY: Cats can wait. And before I know it we are outside.
Well. Thanks for coming for coffee. Yeah. It's been fun. I should go because my Mum and Dad…

ROB: Sure. I suppose we better say goodbye.

POPPY: Yeah.

They sing.

POPPY: He's leaning in near
   I'm filled with fear

ROB: Oh dear

They both lean in but lead the same way and but heads slightly.

POPPY: Sorry.

ROB: No. Sorry. I'm clumsy.

POPPY: It's okay. Erm. You go that way, I'll go this way?

ROB: Got it.

They lean in again.

They sing

ROB: I like her a lot
   Oh she's so hot

The phone goes

POPPY: Or not.
   Damn phone. Sorry. Where were we?

ROB: Just about...

They sing

POPPY: It's happening now

ROB: Not sure I know how

POPPY: Oh wow

They lean into kiss

POPPY'S DAD: Poppy. Is that you love?

ROB: Night then.

   ROB *bottles it and shakes* **POPPY***'s hand.*

POPPY: Night.

We are back in modern day.

SEREN: He actually shook your hand.

POPPY: Yep.

ROB: Okay. I'll admit it wasn't one of my finest moments.

POPPY: I thought it was cute. A bit official but sweet nonetheless.

ROB: Thanks

POPPY: And I'm flopping down on the bed and there's a text message from Rob.

ROB: Thanks for coming out with me.

POPPY: And I'm typing back next time I'll turn my phone off.

ROB: And I'm typing back next time I'll kiss you good-night.

POPPY: And I'm falling asleep smiling.

SCENE 14

MADDIE: Well aren't you super cute. In other news it's Year 10 sex education day and guess who's back?

LUCY: I think I missed that day.

    DANNO *and* **MAXINE** *enter.*

DANNO: That's right. Dan, Dan the man.

MAXINE: Hello.

SALLY: Obviously someone needed some sex education.

MADDIE: And this time they're talking to us about STIs

ALL: That's sexually transmitted infections

MADDIE: And it's super scary.

    MAXINE *and* **DANNO** *get operatically sinister and scary.*

STI Song

MAXINE: If you do not take care
And you do it
Or you are unaware
And the condom splits
Then you should brace yourself for a nasty fright
An STI could kill you in the dead of night!

DANNO: There are many different ones
Each have a risk
Some have no symptoms
Some where you'll itch
You can get lice that live in pubic hair
They'll bite you and they'll lay eggs if you don't take care

DAVID: Eergh that's disgusting.

MAXINE: Chlamydia can be
Got rid of fast
If you take anti bs
Make sure you ask
Your partner's history before you cum
This STI can stop you from ever being a mum

POPPY: Infertile. Oh God.

DANNO: Then there are loads of things
With nasty sores
Blisters or weeping stings inside your drawers.

MADDIE: That's it. I'm never having sex ever.

SEREN: Okay stop this. This is ridiculous.

MAXINE: What?

POPPY: This is important stuff.

ROB: We do need to know the risks.

SEREN: Yeah but the way they're talking you'd think that sex is always a bad thing. If I'd listen to them I'd think that most people were carrying some kind of horrible disease.

DANNO: We're not saying that. We're just saying you can't tell who has and who hasn't so you need to:

A ding is heard.

DANNO: Talk to your partner about their sexual history

A ding is heard.

DANNO: Get tested

A ding is heard.

DANNO AND MAXINE: Use a condom!

SEREN: Yes, we know and we get that but what about all the other stuff.

MAXINE: Other stuff?

SALLY: I went through years 7 to 11 sex education feeling like everyone in whole world is heterosexual.

MAXINE: We did try and include everyone.

DANNO: Some schools weren't very keen. Thought it was a bit much.

MAXINE: They were just a bit worried that, if we told you that stuff, then you might experiment.

ROB: Are you serious?

SEREN: That's ridiculous.

DANNO: They just thought you were a bit young to talk about the gay stuff.

SALLY: How old were you when you first knew you were straight?

MAXINE: I don't know.

ASH: How old were you when you first identified as a man?

DANNO: What?

POPPY: And those aren't the only things. You made it seem like people only have sex when they want to have a baby. It's all sperm meets egg and fallopian tubes but then there's all the other stuff.

ROB: Yeah like how do you know if you're ready?

CHARLOTTE: How often should you…?

MELANIE: Can girls masturbate too?

POPPY: How long should it last?

MIKE: Do I put the condom on or does she put it on for me?

MADDIE: Will it hurt the first time?

DANNO: I'm afraid that's all we've got time for.

MAXINE: Yes, must be going.

(They round on DANNO and MAXINE.)

Sex Isn't Fun

ALL: Is that it?
It's not fair
I knew everything they taught us in there
That's not sex
Or education
I'm staging my personal investigation

They're trying to tell us that sex isn't fun
But I love the buzz in my head when I'm turned on
When I'm turned on
When I'm turned on
When I'm turned on

When girls are turned on blood rushes to their genitals
And makes the labia and vagina wet
It's mainly when they're tense or not turned on
That they might have painful sex

Did you know that the clitoris is there
On all babies in the womb
But as sex is determined
Boys' become penises
News to you I presume

They're trying to tell us that sex isn't fun
But I love the buzz in my head when I'm turned on
When I'm turned on
When I'm turned on
When I'm turned on

Real life's not like porn, foreplay is a must
Make sure you're both relaxed before you
Start to thrust
And the best way to know if your partner's feeling ready
Is to talk, a lot, and always take it steady

Because they're trying to tell us that sex isn't fun
But I love the buzz in my head
When I'm turned on
When I'm turned on
When I'm turned on

SCENE 15

POPPY: So it's year 11 and we're all stressed out of our minds with GCSEs but still school insists on putting in a sex ed day.

Everyone groans.

MADDIE: Like we had any time to do it anyway.

LUCY: I don't think I was in that day.

POPPY: Lucy. Did you ever go to school?

LUCY: Yeah. I just missed those days.

ROB: One day a year to teach us all that stuff just isn't enough.

LUCY: You can say that again.

LUCY *stands up. She is pregnant.*

DAVID: Woah!

SALLY: Why didn't you say anything?

MADDIE: I don't wanna be bitchy or nothing but do you think Lucy's put on weight?

CHARLOTTE: Err Maddie?

MADDIE: What? I'm just saying. Maybe she's been comfort eating because of exam stress. It happens.

CHARLOTTE *whispers in her ear.*

MADDIE: Oooooooohhhhhhhh.

MELANIE: So how far gone are you?

LUCY: I'm due in July.

CHARLOTTE: Least you'll get your exams out of the way.

LUCY: Yeah.

DAVID: You did know though right?

LUCY: What?

DAVID: Where babies come from.

LUCY: Yeah. I just didn't think it would happen to me. We only did it a few times and he promised to pull out before he actually ejaculated.

MADDIE: Oh yeah, that doesn't work 'cause you can get sperm in the fluid that sometimes comes out before they ejaculate.

LUCY: Thanks for the heads up.

MADDIE: Basically you can get pregnant every time, in any position unless you use contraception and even then it's not 100%.

LUCY: Really!

MADDIE: Sorry. I was just sayin'.

LUCY: I've got to go. I've got a scan.

MADDIE: Oh, okay bye.

SCENE 16

SEREN: Even those of us who went to the sex ed days still had lots of questions that didn't get answered. Maybe if we'd talked about that stuff then he wouldn't...it wouldn't...you know...

POPPY: We don't have to do this bit.

DAVID: If it's too much we can skip it.

SEREN: No. It's important. We need to tell it.

POPPY: Shall we tell it together.

SEREN: Okay.

POPPY: Okay.

    TIM *appears.*

TIM: Okay.

DAVID: What's he doing here?

SEREN: They need to hear his side of it too.

POPPY: Are you sure about this?

    SEREN *ignores her and picks up the story.*

SEREN: So it's year 11. We're at a party at David's house

DAVID: My parents are away so I put out a message

SEREN: Open House.

DAVID: Party time

TIM: So I'm getting there early. Take over some beers. Chill out. Play some Xbox.

DAVID: I'm not drinking 'cause I'm wanting a clear head. My parents will kill me if the place gets wrecked and Poppy says Seren is coming and I don't want to show myself up.

SEREN: I'm going to Poppy's to get ready, plan our outfits, do our hair.

POPPY: Her Dad would never let her go to David's without adults there so she's staying over at mine and they won't know.

SEREN: Poppy is doing my make up

POPPY: And I'm lending her a dress because her stuff

SEREN: Well it's not exactly

POPPY: Flattering and she's super pretty and I want her to have a great time.

SEREN: And I'm showing her the bottle I've taken from my Dad's cabinet.

POPPY: And she's handing me the bottle and I'm taking a swig.

And she's tipsy now. Not drunk drunk. Just a bit more relaxed and…

SEREN: Poppy's telling me to save some for the party and she's putting the bottle in her bag.

POPPY: And my Dad's driving us to the party.

SEREN: And there's lots of people there. Some people from school

POPPY: Some people we know and some people we don't but the music is too loud to talk to anyone any way so…

SEREN: A bunch of girls are dancing and we're joining in…

DAVID: And it's going well. It's a good party. People are having a good time.

TIM: And it's then that I spot Seren. I've seen her at school and I like her. She seems nice and she's really pretty…

SEREN: And that guy Tim's here and he starts dancing too

DAVID: And Tim's really wasted now and he's making a total prat of himself.

SEREN: ...And a couple of people laugh because well it's Tim but I think they're being harsh so I'm beckoning him over.

TIM: And she's smiling at me and calling me over and I know some people are sniggering but I've had some beers so I don't care and I'm showing her my moves.

SEREN: And he's cutting some pretty weird shapes but I think he's funny so I'm doing the same

POPPY: And Tim and Seren are doing all these crazy dance moves and we're all joining in.

DAVID: Everyone's doing it and I don't know who starts it but someone coins the move as doing a 'Tim' and we are all chanting his name as he takes centre stage.

TIM: And she's calling out my name and she's laughing and smiling and she is so fit so I take her hand and pull her to me and I'm kissing her cheek and she's not stopping me.

SEREN: And I'm bumping against him and his lips touch my cheek. It's kind of sloppy but everyone makes a massive deal so....

DAVID: I can't believe she's letting Tim do that to her.

SEREN: I don't want to hurt his feelings so I'm trying to manoeuvre myself to make sure it doesn't happen again and I'm turning around...

POPPY: Seren's acting really out of character and she's showing off to Tim and dancing around.

TIM: And she is seriously stunning and she's kind of circling her hips at me so I reach out and...

SEREN: Tim's grabbing me now and he won't let go..

TIM: And I'm holding her close and she's loving it

SEREN: And I'm hating it

TIM: And I can feel her pressing up against me

SEREN: And I can feel him pressing up against me as I struggle to get away and I'm trying to catch Poppy's eye

POPPY: Why's she looking at me? And it's then I realise she's not having a good time so I'm storming right in there.

Seren, we've got to go. Your Dad just called. We have to go home! I'm lying but it doesn't matter. And she's annoyed for a while 'cause I gave her a fright but mainly she's grateful 'cause I gave her a way out.

SEREN: But that isn't what happened.

POPPY: I know but I wish that it was. And I'm wondering why she is looking at me. I'm so embarrassed so I'm turning away and I'm going outside to talk to Rob

SEREN: And she's disappearing.

TIM: And I'm taking her hand and I'm whispering 'Come upstairs'

SEREN: And he's slurring something into my ear and I don't hear it so I'm just nodding and smiling and he's pulling me by my arm and somehow we're heading up the stairs when…

DAVID: Seren, Seren, are you okay?

SEREN: What? Erm David errr….

DAVID: And she doesn't look right. Her eyes are all glazed and she's stumbling so… Sorry buddy no one's allowed upstairs. House rules.

TIM: Oh come on. We won't make a mess..

DAVID: Sorry. I promised my mum. And Tim's getting lairy now and he keeps holding onto Seren but I can tell from her face that she's not happy about it so I'm taking him to one side and I'm having a word with him but he isn't backing down so I'm shouting in his face and things are getting physical and I'm pushing him away and I'm saving her and she's so grateful to be saved.

SEREN: But that isn't what happened

DAVID: I know. But it could have been. If I'd only seen what was happening right in front of my face.

SEREN: And somehow we're heading up the stairs…

DAVID: And I'm seeing Tim taking her up the stairs and I can't believe she's going with him. I can't believe I liked her. She'd barely even spoken to Tim before tonight and now they're heading upstairs. What a slut. And I decide to give up on not drinking and I'm grabbing a beer.

SEREN: And we're in a bedroom now and it must be David's little sister's 'cause there's cuddly toys everywhere and I am wishing I was at home in my bedroom and that I'd never come out. I'm wishing I was seven years old again. And he's putting a chair against the door so I can't get out.

TIM: And I'm putting a chair against the door so no one comes in.

SEREN: And he's looking at me and he's realising I'm not into this and I want to go downstairs and he's upset with himself for misreading the situation but I'm telling him its alright and we're hugging it out.

TIM: But that isn't what happened.

SEREN: I know. But I wish it was.

TIM: And I don't know what I'm doing…

SEREN: I don't know what he's doing…

TIM: So I just sort of go for it.

SEREN: And he's pushing me on the bed as the fear fills me up

TIM: And I'm pushing her on the bed as the passion takes over and it's just like I've seen online only better…

SEREN: And it's not like how it seems in films. It's much, much worse. And I can't believe this is happening…

TIM: And I can't believe this is happening. And I'm hoping I'm doing it okay and I'm closing my eyes and concentrating so it's not over too quickly…

SEREN: And I'm closing my eyes and I'm willing it to be over. My mind is disconnecting from my body and I'm just lying here and switching off the pain. I think about screaming but no sound comes out and then it's over…

TIM: I've finished and I don't know what to say. Suddenly I'm feeling self conscious and I want to talk to her. I'm wanting to ask her if she had a good time but no words come out so I'm just kissing her on the cheek and I'm leaving the room.

SEREN: And just like that he's going like nothing has happened and I'm wanting to get out of here and when I'm getting myself together and I'm worried because Poppy's dress is a bit ripped and she'll kill me if she sees....

(A couple of drunkard girls come in.)

MELANIE: Whoops. Sorry.

SALLY: Oh my God. Are you okay?

SEREN: And I'm hearing myself say, 'yeah, I'm fine' and I'm running downstairs and going to find Poppy...

POPPY: And Seren finally is bothered to find me

SEREN: And I'm saying I want to go...

POPPY: But I'm not letting her ruin my night and she's staying over at mine so...

SEREN: She wants to stay so I'm pretty much stuck and I don't tell her what has happened....

TIM: And I can't believe what just happened so I start telling Dave and he makes a massive deal out of it..

DAVID: I can't believe Tim and Seren just did the nasty in my little sister's room. I can't believe Tim has actually lost his virginity so I'm slapping him on the back and telling everyone who'll listen.

SEREN: And everyone at the party is staring at me and whispering until Poppy's dad comes to get us and we go home.

Back in the modern day.

POPPY: Why didn't you say anything?

SEREN: I was probably in shock. I thought if I didn't talk about it, it might not be real.

DAVID: I wouldn't have told everyone if I'd realised.

SEREN: But you knew what people were like. Even if I had been happy to do it. It would have still been me everyone was gossiping about while Tim gets some kind of gold medal.

DAVID: I'm really sorry.

POPPY: We didn't know.

SEREN: At first I was just numb and then the numbness turned into anger. About a week later my sister came to visit and the whole thing came out.

SCENE 17

TIM: So I'm sat at home on a Sunday and Mum's in the kitchen when the doorbell goes and I'm expecting it to be David or Mike seeing if I want to go for a bike ride but it's not David or Mike.

POLICE M: Are you Timothy White?

TIM: Yeah

POLICE M: Can we come in? Are your parents home?

TIM: And two police officers are coming into my house and mum's coming out of the kitchen and she's looking really scared.

SEREN: If I tell you something do you promise to keep it a secret?

CARYL: That depends what it is.

SEREN: Please Caryl.

CARYL: Come on. Tell me. You know you can trust me.

SEREN: You can't tell Dad.

CARYL: Just tell me.

POLICE M: Timothy White. We have reason to believe that last Saturday night you attended a party at David Gulliver's House. I'm arresting you on suspicion of raping Seren Hughes at that party.

MUM: Rape!

POLICE M: You do not have to say anything but it may harm your defense if you do not mention when questioned something you later rely on in court, anything you do say may be given in evidence.

TIM: I didn't Mum.

POLICE M: We are going to take you to the station for questioning.

POLICE W: Are you his mum? Can you come with him?

MUM: What? Yes. This is a mistake.

POLICE W: What were you wearing that night Tim?

TIM: I don't remember.

MUM: You had on those black jeans and that green shirt.

POLICE W: Have those items been washed?

TIM: I don't know.

MUM: I think they're still in the basket. Tim. Go and get them.

TIM: What? You can't be...

MUM: Look this is obviously a mistake. You need to co-operate as fully as possible till this whole thing is over and they realise they've made a mistake.

POLICE M: My colleague will come with you. We'll need to bag up everything including your underwear as evidence.

TIM: And I'm heading upstairs with this police woman with a plastic evidence bag and I'm giving her my clothes and I can hear my mum crying downstairs and I can't believe this is really happening. My mind is disconnecting from my body as they're leading us out and Mum is gripping my hand and telling me it's going to be alright.

SEREN: A couple of weeks ago I went and stayed at Poppy's except I didn't just stay at Poppy's...we went to a house party.

CARYL: Whose house?

SEREN: David. I don't think you know him.

CARYL: Okay.

SEREN: And I took some alcohol from Dad's cabinet.

CARYL: Ok.

SEREN: What do you mean ok?

CARYL: Well I'd rather you hadn't but its not exactly the crime of the century...

SEREN: I'd drunk quite a bit of it before we got to the party.

CARYL: Right.

POLICE W: Talk us through the events of Saturday night Tim.

TIM: I got to the party around 7. Played some X box with David. After a bit Mike showed up.

POLICE W: Were you drinking?

TIM: ...

MUM: Just tell the truth.

TIM: We had some beers.

SEREN: When we got there, I was up for having a good time and everyone was dancing....

CARYL: Were you sick?

SEREN: No.

CARYL: Well you're one up on me. The first time I had a drink I threw up all over that boy Kevin Spencer. Do you remember him?

SEREN: Was he the one with the glasses and the mac?

CARYL: That's the one.

SEREN: Was he wearing the mac at the time?

CARYL: Sadly not.

Silence.

CARYL: So what happened?

SEREN: This guy Tim was there and he kept dancing with me and pushing up against me…

CARYL: And you didn't like it.

SEREN: No.

TIM: The party started getting busier. Lots of people arrived and started dancing.

POLICE W: Okay, and what time did Seren arrive?

TIM: I don't remember. Maybe it was 9 when I saw her dancing but I'm not sure.

MUM: Just do your best love.

POLICE W: How did she seem?

TIM: She seemed happy. She was all dressed up and she was dancing with Poppy.

POLICE M: Do you know her well?

TIM: A bit. We're not in the same sets.

POLICE M: Would you consider her your girlfriend?

TIM: No.

POLICE M: Did you see her drinking alcohol?

TIM: No.

POLICE M: Did she look like she'd been drinking alcohol before she arrived?

TIM: No. I don't know. Maybe?

POLICE W: And what happened next?

TIM: And I'm telling them about dancing with her and messing around and kissing her and everyone cheering and they keep asking me the same kind of questions.

POLICE W: Did you think that Seren wanted to be kissed?

TIM: I don't know. She was smiling so I guess so. Yes.

POLICE W: Did she like it when you were dancing close to her?

TIM: Yeah. She was kind of rubbing against me so…

POLICE M: Do you think it was possible that she was trying to get away?

TIM: I didn't think so.

POLICE W: How were you holding her?

TIM: I had my arms around her waist.

POLICE W: And was she facing you?

TIM: No. She'd turned away.

POLICE W: So you were facing each other but after you kissed her she turned away from you?

TIM: I suppose so. When you say it like that it sounds…it doesn't sound right…she was into it. I could tell.

CARYL: So what happened?

SEREN: I don't know. It doesn't matter. I'm not sure. Everything is a bit of a blur.

CARYL: Seren. Tell me.

SEREN: He pulled me upstairs …

CARYL: And you didn't want to go with him?

SEREN: No.

CARYL: What was everyone else doing? Where was Poppy?

SEREN: They were dancing or drinking. She'd gone outside I think…

CARYL: And just left you there?

SEREN: There were loads of us there. He took me upstairs and put a chair against the door…

CARYL: Oh God.

SEREN: And then he…we…well you know…

TIM: I asked her if she wanted to go upstairs. I wasn't sure if she heard me at first because the music was loud but then she smiled so we went upstairs.

MUM: Oh God.

TIM: I'm sorry Mum.

POLICE W: Are you sure she heard what you'd said?

TIM: I thought so.

POLICE W: You see Tim. You need to be sure that the girl you're having sex with gives you her consent before you do anything. That means that she has to have said yes.

TIM: Right.

POLICE W: Did she say yes Tim?

TIM: She didn't say no.

POLICE M: What happened next?

TIM: We went up the stairs.

CARYL: Seren. You have to tell me exactly what he did.

SEREN: He had sex with me.

CARYL: And you didn't want him to?

SEREN: No.

POLICE M: Did Seren seem drunk?

TIM: Yeah, I think so. I was holding onto her because she was a bit wobbly.

MUM: Look. They're just a couple of stupid drunk teenagers who have obviously done something stupid. That doesn't make my son a rapist.

POLICE M: If Seren was too drunk to give her consent and your son had sex with her then the law counts that as rape.

MUM: I can't believe this is happening.

CARYL: Do you realise what you're saying here? You're saying you've been raped.

SEREN: This is why I didn't tell you. I knew you'd overreact.

CARYL: I'm not overreacting. If someone has sex with you and you haven't given your permission, that's rape.

SEREN: But I was dancing with him.

CARYL: So what. That doesn't mean he had the right to have sex with you.

SEREN: What if I led him on? I was wearing Poppy's dress and it was really short…

CARYL: It doesn't matter if you were dancing around completely naked. It didn't give him the right to have sex with you if you didn't want it.

SEREN: But I was drunk.

CARYL: If you'd had too much to know what you were doing then you weren't in a fit state to give consent. That counts as rape.

SEREN: I didn't say no.

CARYL: Did you say yes?

SEREN: No.

CARYL: Then that's all that matters.

SEREN: I didn't scream.

CARYL: Oh sweetheart. It's okay. Come here. We'll get through this. I've got you.

TIM: We went into David's sister's bedroom and …

POLICE W: And..

TIM: I put a chair against the door.

MUM: Tim!

TIM: I didn't want anyone coming in.

POLICE M: And once you were in the bedroom?

TIM: We kind of fell on the bed and I was kissing her.

POLICE W: Was she kissing you back?

TIM: No. I don't think so.

POLICE M: Did the two of you talk?

TIM: No. We just…just…we just had sex.

POLICE W: Were you looking at her face while you were having sex with her.

TIM: No. I had my eyes closed.

POLICE W: And was she moving or giving you any indication that she liked what was happening?

TIM: She wasn't screaming.

POLICE W: And when the sex was finished, did you talk then?

TIM: I didn't know what to say. So I just kissed her and went downstairs.

SEREN: So my sister takes me to a sexual assault referral centre. I'm thinking it's nice in a screwed up sort of way and I'm giving them Poppy's ripped dress.

And it's all women and they are being really kind to me.

And I'm explaining what happened and I'm giving them samples.

TIM: And they're making me give samples.

SEREN: And they're arranging for me to be examined and I'm crying as it happens.

And they are believing me and I don't feel so frightened any more and I'm deciding to report it.

TIM: And I am realising that I have made the biggest mistake of my life.

A moment out of time.

TIM: I pleaded guilty.

SEREN: I know.

TIM: Tried to face up to what had happened.

SEREN: What were you thinking?

TIM: I don't know. I just felt really very confused and frightened.

SEREN: Even though you moved schools your shadow was everywhere.

TIM: Do you hate me?

SEREN: I did then.

TIM: And now?

SEREN: No. To hate you would mean using feelings on you and I'm not letting you have that power. You're just some stupid boy who did a horrible, wicked, messed up thing that I'm going to have to live with for the rest of my life.

TIM: I'm sorry. That's what I imagine saying to you if I ever see you again.

SEREN: But that's not what happened.

TIM: I know.

SCENE 18

POPPY: Year 12.

ROB: Sixth form

POPPY: Rob and me. We're still together.

ASH: And people are starting to grow up a bit. They're not giving me quite such a hard time.

POPPY: Mike's going out with Maddie!

MADDIE: No need to say it like that.

ROB: We all just thought he'd get married to his right hand.

    ASH *laughs.*

POPPY: What? I don't get it.

ROB: I love you.

POPPY: What?

ASH: Don't let me get in the middle of a…

ROB: Nothing.

POPPY: Robert Godfrey Somers tell me what you just said.

ASH: *(Laughing.)* Godfrey?

ROB: It's a family name.

POPPY: I'm waiting.

ROB: Nothing. I didn't say anything.

POPPY: *(Dejected.)* Oh, right. Obviously you didn't mean…

ROB: I did. I mean, hypothetically if I had said something and hypothetically if I had have meant it. Would you mind?

POPPY: Well hypothetically…

MADDIE: Oh for goodness sake. He said he loves you Poppy. Now can you just love him back already 'cause this is really annoying.

POPPY: Did ya?

ROB: Yeah. Do you?

POPPY: Yeah.

ASH: Now will you just get on with the play!

ROB: So Mike's with Maddie and things seem pretty serious.

MADDIE: And I really thought things were going well. He'd grown up a bit, we all had.

SCENE 19

MADDIE: Once you get through all that macho stuff Mike's a really nice guy.

MIKE: And once you get past all her gossiping she's a really great girl. She's funny, and kind and seriously sexy.

MADDIE: And he's actually a surprisingly good listener and an amazing kisser.

SALLY: Mike?

MADDIE: Yep, you's missin' out.

SALLY: I'm alright thanks mate.

MADDIE: So it when he asked me for a picture. It wasn't like other guys. I'd been staying over at his and we'd had the most perfect weekend.

MIKE: I just want to be able to look at you when we're not together.

MADDIE: How can I be sure that you're not going to go passin' it around?

MIKE: As if. Why would I do that? You and me babes. It's our thing. I don't want anyone else involved.

And I meant it. Some things are private.

MADDIE: And he made me feel really beautiful and I trusted him so...

MIKE: Just one teeny tiny pic?

MADDIE: Alright then.

He takes the photo.

MIKE: And I really meant what I said. Things moved pretty fast after that and they were going really well until.

SCENE 20

MIKE *and* **MADDIE** *are in bed. Things have clearly not gone well.*

MADDIE: It's okay.

MIKE: It's not.

MADDIE: It's not a big deal.

MIKE: It is.

MADDIE: It's understandable. You're nervous. Everyone gets nervous. Today just wasn't the day. We can just try again another time.

MIKE: ...

MADDIE: Oh come on. Don't be all sulky.

MIKE: I've ruined it.

MADDIE: You haven't. You can't ruin us just because it didn't work out this time.

MIKE: The first time. The one you're meant to remember for the rest of your life and I've completely blown it.

MADDIE: You haven't. Okay so this isn't the first time 'cause we haven't actually done it yet...

MIKE: Thanks. I hadn't noticed.

MADDIE: I just mean they'll be another chance okay? You're still you and I'm still me and I'm still really into you and… Mike? You do still want us to don't you…?

MIKE: Yeah.

MADDIE: You don't sound too convinced. Is it me? Is my body not what you were expecting or not you're thing…

MIKE: No! You're perfect. Beautiful. I just feel like I've let you down.

MADDIE: You haven't. Come here you big brown bear…

MIKE: Stop it.

MADDIE: Say it.

MIKE: You're my fluffy bunny wunny.

They snuggle.

SCENE 21

MIKE: And I was really thankful that Maddie didn't make a big deal out of it. Honestly, I didn't really know what the problem was. It didn't happen when I was watching stuff on my own just when she was there but I really liked her and then, and this is the really embarrassing bit….

MIKE *settles down to pleasure himself.*

MADDIE: Mike. Mike. Your Mum let me in.

MIKE: Hold on.

MADDIE: What are you up to in there?

MIKE: Wait!

MADDIE *has walked in on* **MIKE** *having a wank.*

MADDIE: What are you doing?

MIKE: *(Too quickly.)* Nothing.

MADDIE: Looks like it.

MIKE: I wasn't.

MADDIE: Calm down.

MIKE: I didn't know you were coming over.

MADDIE: Clearly. *(She presses up against him.)* But now that I am here it seems a waste not to take advantage.

She leads him into the bed.

MADDIE: You were obviously having a good time so let's have a good time together.

They disappear under the covers.

MIKE: Maddie. Just wait. Can you…

MADDIE: Right. Fine.

MIKE: Look. It's not you. Okay. This is my problem.

MADDIE: Well it didn't seem like a problem before I got here.

MIKE: Look honestly…

   MADDIE *grabs the mobile.*

MADDIE: What have they got that I haven't?

MIKE: Nothing. You're perfect.

MADDIE: I'm perfect. So perfectly perfect that you'd rather get off to some girls online than with me.

MIKE: I wouldn't.
   I don't know why this is happening.
   I'm not making it happen.
   This doesn't change the way I feel about you.

MADDIE: Well it changes the way I feel about you.

MIKE: Maddie. Don't be like that. Please.

MADDIE: You and me babes. We're finished.

   MADDIE *exits.*

MIKE: I just don't understand why this is happening to me.

DANNO *and* **MAXINE** *appear.*

MAXINE: Perhaps we can help.

MIKE: Okay this is getting seriously weird now.

DANNO: We can explain.

MAXINE: I think I feel another song coming on?

Dopamine, Dopamine ra ra ra

ALL: Dopamine dopamine rah rah rah
Dopamine dopamine rah rah rah
Dopamine dopamine rah rah rah
Dopamine dopamine rah rah rah

MAXINE: I know you're wondering why you can't get it up.

DANNO: You've been putting too much dopamine in your cup.

MAXINE: Also referred to as the happy chemical
It's that feeling you get when you're busy having sex

DANNO: But also when you run

DANNO and MAXINE: Or eat a sticky bun

ALL: Dopamine dopamine rah rah rah
Dopamine dopamine rah rah rah

DANNO: The thing about a good thing is you just want more
And you flood your brain with dopamine when you're watching porn

MAXINE: Trouble is in real life you're with another person
They have feelings and needs
And you want to succeed
But the pressure is massive and you end up being flaccid

ALL: Dopamine dopamine rah rah rah
Dopamine dopamine rah rah rah
Dopamine dopamine rah rah rah
Dopamine dopamine rah rah rah

DANNO: The more you get, the more you need
That's the wicked thing about dopamine

MAXINE: So you're looking for a buzz in someone else's hands
Want a real relationship but not sure if you can

DANNO: I mean you want this girl, it's not going to plan
You need to find a way to feel like a real man

MAXINE: They do it on film but porn isn't fact

DANNO: You need to switch it off and take your real life back

ALL: Dopamine dopamine rah rah rah
Dopamine dopamine rah rah rah

DANNO: Masturbation is healthy and normal and real

MAXINE: Unlike on that film where the girls pretend to feel.

DANNO: So if you're watching too much you might get stuck
With a girl, on your own, you think that you're in luck
There's a kiss, a snog, it soon becomes a touch
You find you're not feeling much......

MAXINE: And if you can't get it up, you certainly can't *(beep)*.

ALL: Dopamine dopamine rah rah rah
Dopamine dopamine rah rah rah
Dopamine dopamine rah rah rah
Dopamine dopamine rah rah rah

    MAXINE and **DANNO** *disappear with the dopamine singers.*

DAVID: So actually watching too much porn can make it harder to have sex?

MIKE: Yep. Who knew...?

DAVID: That's why I've cut it out.

ASH: Serious?

MIKE: I really am trying to sort it out.
    I think maybe watching that stuff as much as I did changed the way
    I looked at girls.

MADDIE: No! Really. We'd never have noticed. Go on. Tell everyone.

MIKE: What?

MADDIE: Come on big man. Tell them what you did.

MIKE: Do I have to?

Under the weight of peer pressure **MIKE** *gives in.*

SCENE 22

MIKE: So Maddie's just walked out on me and I'm feeling embarrassed and upset and angry. And I'm thinking how could she and is she going to tell anyone and what will my mates say. And it's like the pressure's building up and something bursts in my brain and I'm opening her picture on my phone and I'm pressing upload.

And I sit there for a moment and I can't believe I just did that. I feel excited and powerful and guilty all at the same time.

ASH: I can't believe you did that!

MIKE: I know alright. I know.

ROB: And you decided the way to win her back was to stick her photo online?
What's wrong with you?

MIKE: I don't know. Once I'd stopped being angry I started feeling really bad about it.

MADDIE: Ha! *You* felt bad about it?!

MIKE: I really am sorry.

MADDIE: Do you have any idea what it was like for me?

MIKE: I know.

MADDIE: I don't think you do actually.

So I get into school the next day and I'm annoyed with myself for having a go at Mike. I'm not stupid. I know boys watch that stuff. It just made me feel inferior and it pushed my buttons. But I'm thinking

I should talk with him and clear the air. But, as I'm walking down the corridor, something don't feel right and I'm thinking am I being paranoid or are people looking at me and whispering?

And people start saying stuff.

KID 4: Alright Maddie.

KID 5: Looking good.

MADDIE: And I'm thinking something is definitely not right and then Charlotte finds me and is taking me to one side.
And I feel embarrassed.

SALLY: You shouldn't. You've got a great body.

MADDIE: I'm not ashamed of my body. That's not the point.
I want to get to decide who sees it. I mean seriously. Hands up who's seen me topless. Come on.

Gingerly all the hands go up.

MADDIE: And if everyone has something it becomes completely worthless.

MIKE: *(Quietly.)* You're not worthless.

MADDIE: Be quiet. I'm talking. I trusted him and, since then, it's been really hard to trust anyone.

SALLY: Did you tell anyone?

MADDIE: Looks like you all knew.

SALLY: I mean parents, teachers, the police. You do know that what he did was illegal?

MADDIE: Yep but what I did was illegal too. Technically I colluded in making child pornography.

SALLY: Okay but they could have helped you get it down.

MADDIE: Yeah, they could.

MIKE: I took it down.

MADDIE: Yep, but once something like that is out there, there's no way to know who made a copy. I'm constantly freaking out now that every new person I meet will have seen it and if I make new friends at uni and they find out then they'll make assumptions about me.

And I'm anxious and nervous and upset all the time and that ain't me babes. He did that to me.

She is upset.

MIKE: I'm guessing you don't want to give us another try?

MADDIE: Errrr thanks but no thanks. I'm a strong independent woman. I'm not gonna have sex until I find someone worth having sex with. I don't need no man and, if I did, it most certainly wouldn't be you.

CHARLOTTE: Ha. You tell him.

DAVID: Poppy, do you think, if I asked her, maybe Seren would want to have a coffee with me?

POPPY: Are you saying does your mate fancy me?

DAVID: No…but does she…?

POPPY: You could ask Seren yourself.

SEREN *arrives.*

SEREN: Ask me what?

DAVID: Oh God. Erm Hi. I just thought …I just wondered…if you're not too busy…maybe…

SEREN: Yes.

DAVID: What?

SEREN: I would like to go out with you. Please pick me up at 7.30pm on Friday. We're going to Nando's.

DAVID: Seriously. I mean yeah that's cool babe. Whatever. *(Quietly and subtly punching the air.)* Yess.

SEREN *leaves and* **DAVID** *follows hers.*

POPPY: Ahhh. Young love eh?

ROB: Now we just have to set you up.

ASH: No need.

ROB: Oh please we'll find you a nice girl..

POPPY: Or a guy if that's your thing.

Enter **CHARLOTTE**.

CHARLOTTE: Ash you coming?

ASH: Just a sec babe.

POPPY: You and Charlotte?

ROB: I did not see that coming.

CHARLOTTE: Well after all the crap I'd been through, I thought it was time I dated a real man.

POPPY *and* **ROB** *stand and hold hands.*

ASH: Well these two are nauseatingly cute aren't they.

ROB: What?

POPPY: I don't know what you mean.

ASH: You're obviously dying to tell everyone about your first time.

ROB: Not particularly.

POPPY: Oh alright then.

ROB: What?

SCENE 23

POPPY: It's year 13.

MADDIE: Year 13?

ROB: We wanted to wait till we were sure.

ASH: But you guys definitely made it seem like..

POPPY: We just didn't want everyone on our backs.

ROB: We wanted to take things at our own pace.

ASH: Fair enough.

POPPY: It was exactly how we'd planned it.

Consent Song

ROB: I can't believe we're here
And now we're so near
I'm filled up with fear
Can I whisper something in your ear

ROB: Would you like a cup of tea?

POPPY: We'll see

ROB: Or some juice in a glass

POPPY: I'll pass

ROB: My room's such a mess

POPPY: No stress

ROB: God I'm such a blabbering fool

BOTH: Oh you're so beautiful
This feels like a musical
God you're so fit
I can't believe it
Can I give you a kiss
But only if you're ok with this.
And sorry if this sounds corny
But you make me feel so…happy

CHORUS:
I just wanna pleasure you
But only if you want it too
I just wanna pleasure you
But only if we've thought this through
I just wanna pleasure you
Let's make like Sims and just woohoo

I just wanna pleasure you tonight
But only if it's alright

ROB: Does your bra undo?

POPPY: For you

ROB: Babe are you sure?

POPPY: Yes more.
I'm loving your touch. So much.

ROB: Can you tell me if it's too much?

POPPY: Sorry about the hair.

ROB: Don't care.

POPPY: Does this feel alright?

ROB: Not quite.

POPPY: How about now?

ROB: Oh wow

BOTH: Together we will learn how
Tell me what you want me to do to you

CHORUS: Oh you're so beautiful
This feels like a musical
God you're so fit
I can't believe it

POPPY: Can we go all the way?

ROB: Oh babe you know it's okay.

POPPY: And sorry if this sounds corny
But you make me feel so…good

CHORUS: I just wanna pleasure you
But only if you want it too
I just wanna pleasure you
But only if we've thought this through

I just wanna pleasure you
Can I Netflix and chill with you.
I just wanna pleasure you tonight
But only if it's alright

EPILOGUE

DAVID: We were the class of 2019.

MADDIE: And this was sex education with a difference.

SEREN: Because there's a bit more to it than sperm meets egg.

ASH: And sex gets serious

DAVID: If you do it too young

LUCY: Or you don't play it safe.

MIKE: Or you believe online stuff is real

MADDIE: Or you're with the wrong one

TIM: Or they haven't said yes.

SALLY: But falling in love is the best feeling

MELANIE: And sex *is* fun.

CHARLOTTE: If you're old enough.

LUCY: And you use contraception.

ASH: And you have trust in your relationship

DAVID: And you're with the right one

SEREN: And you have both said yes.

    ROB *and* **POPPY** *are dishevelled and red faced following the act of coitus.*

POPPY: Do you want to go again?

ROB: Maybe give me a chance to recover.

    Black out.